Food Truck Funding with Kickstarter

How to Use Crowdfunding to Generate Startup Capital

By Andrew Moorehouse

A Free Gift for You

As a thank you for your purchase, I'm making my book **Food Truck Vehicles and Equipment** available to you for free.

You'll get an introduction to food trucks and the vehicles used in the industry. In this booklet, you can find some basic costs of buying a food truck and learn about what food truck builders can do for you.

Visit the URL below for this exclusive offer:

TheFoodTruckStartup.com/free

Books Available in the
Food Truck Startup Series

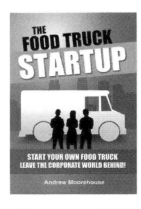

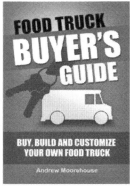

TABLE OF CONTENTS

Introduction

If you've ever dreamed of starting your own food truck business, be ready for an experience that will challenge you to the extremes and also create satisfaction like nothing else! If you were to ask random business owners, you'll find that there are endless stories of early struggles just to make it to launch day. But how do everyday people accomplish such a goal? Business owners come from all types of industries and backgrounds. Most of them start their own businesses to achieve the freedom to work for themselves. This freedom often means independence, greater earning potential and a sense of fulfillment that can only come from building a successful business.

One of the industries that can offer all that and more is the mobile food industry! The popularity of gourmet food trucks has exploded for both consumers and owners. In fact, food truck programs on television are further fueling the interest in this fast growing and profitable industry. If you've watched these programs or experienced the excitement around mobile kitchens in person, then you can see why so many people are turning to the streets to create their next business.

To start a business, you need adequate funding. And just as the mobile food industry sets the trends in high tech food marketing, other high tech industries are helping many food truck owners to generate the capital they need to get their ideas off the ground. Through crowdfunding, a business owner could fully fund or partially fund a project to obtain the capital needed without the hassles of a traditional loan. This is not necessarily a simple task! There are specific guidelines to follow to increase your chances of success. The goal of this book is to show you specific tips you can integrate into your food truck crowdfunding project so you can join the entrepreneurs before you who have obtained startup capital through this innovative funding platform. Let's get started!

-Andrew Moorehouse

Chapter 1 – Introduction to Crowdsourcing

Before we dive into crowdfunding, let's learn about the broader concept of Crowdsourcing first for a better understanding of how it helps people. Crowdsourcing is a new term that you may or may not have heard of but it is gaining popularity in the business world. Crowdsourcing is a form of outsourcing that can be very effective for certain types of goals. At the center of this idea is the concept of utilizing the internet and online tools to tap into the so called "crowds" of people either locally or worldwide to:

Get tasks done

Generate ideas

Get people to take action

In other words, you can obtain the help of large amounts of people from all over the globe to help achieve your goals. Sometimes the help is free, at other times there is a cost but the main thing to remember is that because the assistance is provided by multiple people, you can achieve your goals faster or get better results by utilizing the minds and resources from multiple individuals or entities.

Uses for Crowdfunding

Let's break down these 3 basic objectives mentioned above one by one to see in detail how crowdsourcing applies to various situations. First, we'll explore what type of tasks can be achieved through crowdsourcing. Almost anything that can be outsourced can be crowdsourced. Some of the tasks you can consider are:

Brand Creation
Photography
Translation
Transcription
Logo Design
App Testing
Search Engine Optimization
Software Development
Video Creation

Next, we can use crowdsourcing to gather input from the public to help generate multiple ideas based on your subject. Practical applications of this concept can come in the form of:

Beta Testing Software
Idea Generation
Problem Solving
Product Feedback
Collective Brainstorming
Contests
Research and Development
Questionnaires and Surveys

The final aspect of crowdsourcing is using it to stimulate action. This could be in the form of:

Political Action
Civic Innovation
Global News Gathering
Crisis and Disaster Support
Monetary Contributions
Volunteer Work
Community Improvements

Now that you have a basic introduction to crowdsourcing, we can now focus on its application for generating monetary contributions which is termed crowdfunding.

Does Crowdfunding Work?

The concept of crowdfunding really isn't that new but it is surprising how many people are unaware of this powerful resource. With crowdfunding, a business or organization now has a chance to achieve a funding goal even if denied loans from a financial institution.

And you know what the amazing thing about crowdfunding is? That it <u>actually </u>works! The number of crowdfunding websites on the internet is slowly growing with some in beta testing or with invitation only. Some only cater to specific types of clients or businesses and some ask for a percentage of the company they contribute to.

One of the most popular crowdfunding platforms today is Kickstarter. They've built a great reputation for generating funds for a variety of projects. To help you create a successful funding project for your food truck, the remainder of this book, is going to focus on Kickstarter. Their website can be found at:

Kickstarter.com

Kickstarter was made for creative individuals that need help funding their projects or goals. The way it works is you post a project on their website. It costs you nothing. Once you create your project, you'll need to set up your funding goal... this is the amount of money you need to raise. Next you need to set a deadline of when you want to reach that goal. The duration can be set between 1 to 60 days. During that time, you want to get as many backers as possible to contribute funds to your project.

If the campaign is successful and the monetary goal is reached within the predetermined time frame, the backer's credit cards will be charged immediately and the project owner receives the funds that were pledged. But what happens if the goal is not reached by the deadline? If a project does not get fully funded by the deadline, the backers don't pay anything and the campaign is deemed unsuccessful. Kickstarter explains this as 'all or nothing' funding. But don't let that turn you away. Kickstarter has already helped fund over $10 million dollars in project goals so this is still something definitely worth looking into if you're starting a food truck business.

Another important aspect of Kickstarter is that you get to keep 100% ownership of your project, Kickstarter only keeps a small percentage of the money raised... you keep the rest! Other crowdfunding platforms might require you to sell part ownership of your business to backers and investors.

Crowdfunding for Food Trucks

Kickstarter is an amazing resource for creative entrepreneurs! Look at some examples of successful gourmet food truck campaigns and judge for yourself!

The DipStik Bus in Pueblo, Colorado needed $13,000 to purchase their bus, trailer and fire pits as well as funds to cover the rest of their startup costs and permits. In other words, they were starting completely from scratch as far as funding goes. After running their project for 30 days, they got 44 backers to contribute $13,727!

The Big Wheel Food Truck in Florida needed improvements and retrofitting for an existing food truck before they could open for business. They already had a catering company and wanted to expand into mobile food to reach more customers. They set a goal of $5,500 and when the campaign was over, they raised $6,837.

Daisy Cakes is a mobile cupcake bakery that was looking to transition from mobile to a permanent brick and mortar bakery and cafe so they can serve their cupcakes 7 days a week. The owners had already invested a lot of their own money and turned to crowdfunding to help update and expand their kitchen. Their goal was to raise $20,000 for this project and backers contributed $20,685 to make this campaign a success.

Those are just 3 examples of how crowdfunding helped small businesses achieve their goals. In the next chapter, learn why Kickstarter is good for the food truck industry and why you need to seriously consider it as one of your top resources for funding.

Chapter 2 – What is Kickstarter?

Kickstarter was launched on April 28, 2009 and is a crowdfunding service for creative projects that cover a wide range of topics. Anything in the creative field can be funded through Kickstarter. Kickstarter users include individuals and organizations that have innovative, ambitious and breakthrough ideas that would benefit from the generosity of backers who want to support those projects. According to Kickstarter statistics, there have been over 30,000 successfully funded projects with a total of $350,000,000 distributed to project owners.

Kickstarter can be used for a variety of projects however it cannot be used for any charities, causes, philanthropy or personal financial gain (such as needing $2000 to buy a laptop for school).

Kickstarter also states that their services are "all or nothing" funding. This means that the funding goal (amount of money requested) must be reached in order for funds to be distributed to the project owner. Otherwise, no money will change hands and the project becomes unsuccessful. According to Kickstarter, this provides less risk for everyone and it motivates people on both sides of the funding project. They have found that projects either find immense support or very little support. There's not much in between when it comes to funding projects.

This "all or nothing" policy has proven to work because projects that reach at least 20% of their funding goal early on have an 82% of success. Also, projects that are able to reach 60% of their goal have a 98% of becoming successfully funded. Out of all the funding projects on Kickstarter, an amazing 44% have been successful in raising the money needed in their campaigns. Kickstarter is definitely a resource you should consider when you are in need of funding because you have nearly a 50% chance of success! In this book, we are going to help you increase your chances of success with insight and specific techniques on how to build a successful Kickstarter campaign for your food truck business.

With that said, never has there been a greater opportunity for food truck startups to secure the funding needed to launch a dream career in the mobile food industry! Unless you have loads of cash in the bank or have been approved for a loan in the amount you need to start your food truck, you're going to want to know how Kickstarter can help raise money from mostly strangers on the internet!

Right now, Kickstarter.com is the leading crowdfunding website for a number of reasons. It quickly grew in popularity for a variety of creative projects in various fields. While most projects funded by Kickstarter have relatively conservative funding goals, there are a handful of successfully funded projects that exceed $1 million!

Who Can Use Kickstarter?

To use Kickstarter to help fund a project, there are a number of requirements that need to be satisfied before you can proceed. Not everyone is eligible to start a Kickstarter project. Here is a list of requirements for US residents that must be met:

Must be 18 years or older
Be a permanent US resident
A social security number (or EIN)
U.S. address
U.S. bank account
U.S. state issued ID or driver's license
Major U.S. credit or debit card

At this point the only other country eligible to use Kickstarter for crowdfunding is the UK. UK residents can create Kickstarter projects by fulfilling these requirements:

Must be 18 years or older
A permanent UK resident or a
Legal identity with a Companies House Number
UK address
UK bank account
UK government issued ID, driver's license or passport
Major UK credit or debit card

In addition, all Kickstarter project creators must have an Amazon Payments account. This is required because Amazon Payments is the company that handles and distributes funds for successful campaigns.

Today, Kickstarter has become increasingly useful for a host of business projects. As the business world starts to accept crowdfunding as a viable source of startup capital, it may not be too surprising to see a shift towards crowdfunding as the first choice when it comes to project funding.

One of the first steps to crowdfunding is to have an idea for a business. If you're reading this, you probably already have that idea… starting your own food truck! But before you post a project, let's look at additional Kickstarter requirements.

Clearly Defined Projects

According to Kickstarter, they only fund projects with clear goals. So how do they define clear goals? Kickstarter states that funding is only available for projects that can be actually completed. Not only that, they require that something must be produced at the completion of the project. For some, the produced project could be a film, artwork, invention, software, books and many other items. Funding projects can't be used for on-going projects that are considered open-ended or that require constant updates and/or maintenance.

Projects Must Be Categorized

Every Kickstarter project has to go through an internal review process and be accepted before you can start a campaign. Since Kickstarter's motto is "A funding platform for creative projects", not every project is going to pass Kickstarter's inspection process. Also projects must fit into one of the approved categories that are listed at their site:

Music
Games
Photography
Technology
Dance
Food
Fashion
Art
Publishing
Comics
Design
Theater
Film & Video

Gourmet food trucks definitely fit into their approved categories under "food". And if you search Kickstarter's list of current and past projects, you'll see a number of food truck projects listed there… both successfully funded and not!

As we dive deeper into building a successful Kickstarter campaign for your future food truck business, keep in mind that it will take a lot of work on your part. It may sound like "easy money" but in reality, it is far from that! Realistically, it could take a few weeks just to put together the whole campaign. The various parts of the campaign will involve:

Copywriting
Determining rewards for backers
Video production
Marketing and promotion
Social media

Relationship building
Answering inquiries
Updating your status
Utilizing funds to complete your project
Distributing rewards

On the surface, it looks like a very manageable list... and in a way it is. But to make your campaign a success, you'll need to follow through with every step to make your efforts count! You're in this to generate real money that could make a significant change in your life! As a result, this change could allow you to quit your job, find a new career, create freedom, become an entrepreneur or turn a dream into reality!

Backers and Fees

The people who contribute funds to your project are called backers. Your first backers will usually be your immediate family, friends and acquaintances. Usually after the initial drive to get your first backers, you'll find that some of their friends will jump on and support your project too! In the course of the funding campaign, there will be others who will find your project through social media and become inspired to support you. Others might only want to obtain the reward you are offering. In the end, all these people become additional backers that will help you get closer to your funding goal. Sometimes these backers are just generous people that want to be involved to support someone else's dream and help make it come true!

The great thing about Kickstarter is that project owners get to keep 100% ownership of their project after funding. They do not give up any portion of the project, company or idea to backers.

However, there is a small fee collected by Kickstarter for hosting your campaign. There are actually 2 fees for running a Kickstarter campaign. The two fees go to:

5% - Kickstarter
3-5% - Amazon Payments

The first fee goes to Kickstarter for hosting the project and to help maintain their service. The 2nd fee goes to Kickstarter's payment processor which is Amazon Payments which helps collect and process all the credit cards from backers and then distributes those funds to you.

Chapter 3 – Creating a Kickstarter Account

Because there are quite a few elements to building a Kickstarter project, you will probably need to start planning at least a month or more before you launch your campaign. You do not want to rush through this part because you could jeopardize your success. This is like doing homework or studying for a test. You do not want to wait until the last minute before you hit the books! By being on top of things, you'll automatically build in time to allow for changes and adjustments to your whole campaign before your launch date. And don't forget about Kickstarter's review time on top of the time you've already spent creating your project. The review process can take up to a week! So if you have certain deadlines you want to meet, you'll definitely want to get started planning your project as soon as you can!

Creating a Kickstarter Profile

To begin your Kickstarter project, you'll need to create an account and profile page. This is really easy to set up and a required step. All you need is your name, email and create a password to create your official Kickstarter account. For some project owners, they opt to use a business name instead of a personal name. This can be advantageous because the project can appear to be more credible by having an official business name. If you use a business name, you can still add your own name for a personal touch in your description and video. Using your own name somewhere in your project can help create a better connection with backers looking at your Kickstarter page. That way, viewers of your Kickstarter page can get an idea of the person or people who are actually behind the project.

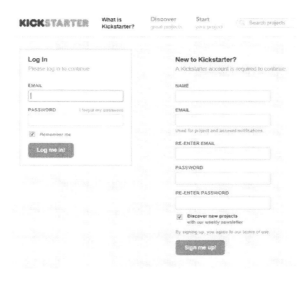

Once you've set up your account, you can begin to build the pieces of your funding campaign. The next thing you want to do is start adding elements to your profile. Uploading a profile image is important because if you don't, your profile image will be represented by a blue square in your bio and other communications within the Kickstarter website.

As a future food truck owner, you can upload a picture of yourself, your food truck logo or a picture of your food truck (with or without a wrap on it). These are going to be the best representations of your business. Just keep in mind that this should be eye-catching. It could be argued that your profile image is the single most important branding aspect of your page! Kickstarter recommends a square image size with equal pixel dimensions on each side. For example, you could use a photo that is 300x300 for uploading to your profile. You can easily crop/resize an image in Photoshop or by using a free image editor called GIMP.

Creating a Bio Page

You'll also want to set up your bio page which tells a little bit more about you or your company. Sometimes a bio is important to backers so that they can get a better idea of who they will be sending funds to… especially if they don't personally know the project owner. The bio page is also where you can provide additional contact information. You can include items like:

Your location
Link to your Facebook page
Link to your website
Link to your Twitter page
Contact me info

In addition to a list of your own projects you've created. This page will also list other Kickstarter projects you have backed.

This list of projects shows that you are active in the Kickstarter community and are willing to give back by helping others. These lists are automatically generated by Kickstarter.

Chapter 4 – Building a Kickstarter Project

Once you have your account and profile information set up, you can begin to build your funding campaign. Hopefully you've done your homework and are prepared with insightful information on these next steps. Start with the main information that is going to go on your Kickstarter project page. This is where good writing skills can come in handy which can definitely have a huge impact on your success!

Choosing a Project Title

Just like a headline in a newspaper or a title of a blog post, your project title is a summary of your project in one short blurb and gives readers a quick idea of what your funds will go towards. If you've ever taken a writing or journalism class, you would know that your title should be very simple, concise and descriptive. The title should contain the name of your food truck and possibly even the words "food truck" in the title itself so that searchers can find your project easily. In general, avoid using words like:

Help
Support
Fund
Need

Those words might indicate to backers that you are a bit needy. Instead, you want to be seen as more appreciative and humble while still being assertive. You don't want backers to think you are just looking to get your hands on their money! Make them feel like they're an integral part of your project! Here are some examples of Kickstarter food truck project titles:

Fueled by Fries: Get Snap's Biodiesel Food Truck on the Road
Renny's Oki Doki Okinawan Food Truck Launch
Seattle's First Paleo Food Truck
Get Lexie's Frozen Custard Truck Rolling

There's really no right or wrong way to title your project but the two most important things for food truck businesses to include are the food truck name and the words "food truck". A good idea would be to come up with several variations and get feedback from friends and family to see what is the most popular title.

Tips for Selecting a Project Image

Your project image is going to be the picture that represents your particular project throughout the Kickstarter website. It will be the thumbnail that appears in the Kickstarter search results and is really the viewer's first impression for your project. If you have a video on your project page, the thumbnail of the video will become your actual project image. Again this image should be bold and memorable. It should invite people to click on your project and read more about it. It's possible that the project image is more effective at getting people to look at your project than the title itself! It can also attract random visitors on the Kickstarter website to actually look at your project and possibly become one of your backers.

So carefully take the time to sort through your images and maybe do some resizing or retouching if you have to before uploading. Kickstarter recommends project images at 640x480 pixels to avoid distortion or unwanted cropping.

Needless to say, your project image needs to be professional looking which helps in your overall credibility. It's amazing that there are still project owners on Kickstarter that use photos that look like amateur snapshots with bad lighting.

Why Create a Brief Description

You will need to come up with a very short, one sentence description of your project. This is not a full description but this text will be used with your project's widget. The widget is a graphical overview that quickly relates information about your project to the Kickstarter audience.

This description needs to be very concise while conveying an effective message. In the examples below you can see how short this message needs to be when someone performs a search query.

In all of the examples, the description is longer than the three lines available for display. Anything longer than about 15 words will be cut off. This doesn't mean that your "short" description can't be longer than 15 words. But knowing this, you just have to include the most compelling information first so it shows up here.

But what happens to the rest of the text that gets cut off? Don't worry! It's still there. If your image, title and short description catch the attention of the reader, they're more inclined to click on your project. When they do, they'll be taken to the actual project page where the "short" description will appear directly under the video or project image.

I know the image is small but look at "The Fiction Kitchen vegetarian restaurant needs equipment!" example above (far right). Their "short" description looks like there are still quite a few words that got cut off. Clicking on their title will take the viewer to the project page where we can see the rest of the text.

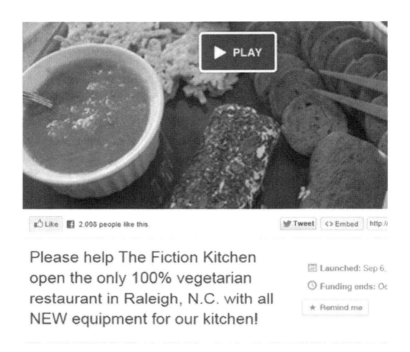

Please help The Fiction Kitchen open the only 100% vegetarian restaurant in Raleigh, N.C. with all NEW equipment for our kitchen!

🗓 Launched: Sep 6,

⏱ Funding ends: Oc

★ Remind me

Writing Your Complete Project Description

Your full project description plays a huge role in convincing backers to support you! It still needs to be fairly short and concise but this is where you can really dive into the details of your project. Think of the project description like a newspaper or magazine article. They're usually not too long but they do provide a lot of information. The five basic principles of journalism apply here:

Who

What

Why

Where

How

Your description does not have to follow in that order but it should follow a similar structure. The beginning of your description should include one or both of these items:

An introduction to the person, team or company
A description of your dream or mission

These items should draw people into your story. The first paragraph should convince people to read your whole project description. Again, take cues from journalists because they use the same tactics to draw you into their articles.

If you don't feel comfortable in your writing skills, continue to write out a few drafts of your description and have friends with writing skills you trust take a look and make suggestions.

Additional Information to Include

After your introduction, you should include some information about your current status. Is your food truck almost ready to hit the road or are you still in the planning stages. Letting people know the progress you've made can help them understand your situation and help convince them to take action.

Include what you need in order to get your food truck on the road. This is where you tell backers where the money will be spent. Do you need funding to buy the truck? Do you need the funds to pay for the truck wrap or kitchen equipment? This is where you will want to include all this type of information. Here's an actual excerpt from a successfully funded project:

"We now need help with the costs of wrapping our truck and purchasing truck appliances! Our truck wrap quote is $5000.00 and we need appliances (commercial slow cooker, French fry cutter and commercial food processor) which total up to $1473.51 after shipping.

The truck wrap is vital to achieving our business goals. Nothing provides more salient marketing opportunities than seeing a beautiful truck on the road. It needs to be loud, bright and attention grabbing. We want everyone to remember the colors and the logo. This is an absolute necessity to assure success in the food truck industry. The commercial appliances hold equal precedence. Commercial graded appliances are specifically designed to handle the high volume production needed to serve more customers (YOU!). This $6473.00 will give us that extra boost we need to brand our truck and get it out on the streets."

As shown in the example, the project owner provides detailed costs and exactly why it is so important for them to obtain the desired funding amount from backers. When backers know this, they can feel confident that their contributions will be put to good use in a business that will be launched in the near future.

Enhancing with Images

Along with the text description, you should include relevant images in your project description. Images enhance and help explain your written story. You do not have to use a lot of images but please include a few you feel are essential to the description. Make sure these photos are professional looking and if possible, crop them and size them the same so they fill the text column fully. The maximum width of your images should be 640 pixels. The pixel height can vary. Of course these should be in JPEG format. The types of images you can include are:

Photos of the owners
Truck images
Logo
Food
Ingredients

You don't have to be limited to the list above but those are only suggestions to get you started. Most likely, those suggestions are all you'll need.

Include a Menu Description

Another component you should add to your Kickstarter project is a partial description of the items you plan on serving. You can and should describe some of your most popular or signature menu items. Include facts such as whether you're using farm fresh ingredients, grass fed beef, organically grown vegetables or gluten-free items just to name a few. Do you have a special technique for preparation or do you offer unique menu items that are not found anywhere else in your city? These are the things you need to consider when writing a menu description.

Chapter 5 – Setting Your Funding Goal

Because Kickstarter's terms indicate that they only provide "all or nothing" funding, you need to carefully decide on a funding goal. The funding goal is ultimately the amount of money you need to complete your project. So before you even create a Kickstarter project, you have to have already gone over your budget and costs so you can come up with a fully researched dollar amount for your goal.

What do you actually need to get your gourmet food truck or cart on the streets and in business? Typical food truck funding requests include:

Truck purchase
Graphic design
Retrofitting
Kitchen equipment
New engine
Vent systems

It's worth noting that most Kickstarter food truck projects are not necessarily used to fully fund the complete startup costs of a mobile food business. Instead, the funds from Kickstarter are usually employed to supplement existing loans and personal monetary contributions already invested into the business.

How Much to Ask For?

With that in mind, funding goals for food truck projects usually fall within the $5,000 to $20,000 range. Also, the higher the funding goal, the more difficult it is to achieve... but not impossible! A goal of $3,000 to $10,000 is the most common for this industry.

Don't get too greedy or you could risk losing the campaign! It is however possible to raise more money than your funding goal. That has happened on many occasions. Sometimes the amount funded is more than double the original goal. But don't get too caught up in that! Reaching your stated funding goal is quite an achievement in itself!

It's worth repeating some of the statistics that were presented at the beginning of this book regarding campaign success. When funding reaches certain milestones, success rates increase. Here are those milestones again:

Reaching 20% funding = 82% success rate
Reaching 60% funding = 98% success rate

Those are incredible figures! If your project reaches just 20% of your funding goal, you have an 82% chance of securing the amount you set for your funding goal! So it's really important when you first launch your project to put a huge amount of effort in reaching that 20% threshold very early on. In a later chapter, you'll learn how to promote your project to increase your chances of success.

What If You Exceed Your Funding Goal?

Reaching a funding goal is exhilarating! However, surpassing your goal is cause for major celebration! Most projects exceed their funding goal by only 1-3%. But there are cases where total funds reached 200%, 300% and even up to 10,000% of the original goal! The last one is not typical but the lower amounts are definitely more realistic.

However, you should absolutely take into account the possibility of this over achievement. So in your project description, you should include a paragraph or two about what you will do with the funds that exceed your goals. Again, this strategy creates confidence with backers and reassures them that you will not squander the extra money.

Setting an Effective Campaign Duration

When you create a Kickstarter project, you need to determine the duration you want it to run. Kickstarter allows you to set your duration for up to 60 days. That may not necessarily sound like a lot of time but it is more than enough to reach your goal. In fact, experts say that 60 days is often too much time! Running a Kickstarter campaign for a longer duration may not necessarily help you achieve your funding goal.

Instead, a shorter duration or deadline can help keep the momentum and energy flowing within your project. Take a look at these mobile food businesses that did not use the maximum allowed duration time:

Cultured Caveman – 130% funded in 2 weeks
Renny's Oki Doki – 227% funded in 2.5 weeks
314 Pie – 123% funded in 30 days
Big Wheel Mobile Food Truck – 124% funded in 30 days
Two Blokes and a Bus - 119% funded in 30 days

The first two mobile businesses in the list reached their goals in about 2 weeks! That is an incredible feat! A more realistic duration to aim for would be 30 days. The majority of successful food truck projects run for 30 days. That is more than enough time if backers are interested in your project.

When to End Your Project

One last thing to consider is your project start and end time. The time of your launch determines when your project will end. For example, if you start your project at 5am, your project is going to end at 5am. This end time is what you need to be concerned about. Chances are that you are not going to be awake at 5am unless you like getting up that early in the morning. But the thing to worry about is that very few if any of your potential backers are going to be awake at that time either!

Instead, consider launching your project at a time when you know you will be awake and can be near a computer. The reason is that you want to be present to monitor and update your project status in those last critical hours… especially if you're just below your funding goal! This way, you can make a last ditch effort to rally your friends and get them to donate those last few dollars to help your project succeed.

Chapter 6 – Creating Your Rewards

One of the critical components that entice backers to support your project is rewards. A reward is what a backer receives when a successful project is completed. It should be emphasized that these rewards should not only be creative but valuable to backers. Backers often make a decision to support projects because of the reward. Do not try to cheat backers by offering low value rewards. They will sense your frugal ways and turn away from your project.

What Type of Rewards to Offer?

Rewards are designed to benefit the backers as much as the project owners. A reward should also be something that is directly produced from the project. That means if your project is an innovative iPhone case, then one of your rewards should be that iPhone case your backers helped to fund. Here's another example. If you're seeking backers for a new music album, then backers should receive a copy of that album when it's completed. Backers want to get something out of their generosity. Here are some common rewards that are offered by project owners:

DVDs
CDs
Tickets
Books
Appearance in a film
Exclusive access
Dining experience
Concerts
Coupons
Gift certificates
Meet a famous person
Meet the inventor
Thank you notes
Name included in credits
Photos

The list can go on and on depending on the output of the final product. After reading your description or watching your video (explained later), backers often look to see the type of rewards listed. Also, rewards need to have a value assigned to them.

How to Price Your Rewards

Each backer is only going to contribute a monetary amount they're comfortable with. That's why you need to set different reward values. With that in mind, not every reward is going to be the same. For example, if you're creating a gadget that is worth $120 retail, you don't want to give that gadget to someone who only contributes $10. Instead, you'd offer a lower value reward for those contributing less.

For a food truck business, you'll have different reward options for backers because you're not creating a physical product. Here are some rewards you could offer for mobile food projects with each value level:

Pledge $5 or more

Thank you email
Hand written thank you note
Facebook recognition

Pledge $10 or more

Bumper sticker
Listed as a backer on food truck website

Pledge $25 or more

2 free meals
Cookbook
Sign your name on back of truck
Coupon book
Hat

Pledge $50 or more

4 free meals
T-shirt
VIP access to skip to the front of the line

Pledge $100 or more

2 Signature condiments and sauces
Autographed T-shirt

Pledge $150 or more

Invitation to grand opening
Full merchandise package (hat, t-shirt, condiments)

Pledge $250 or more

Catered lunch for 6 people
1 hour cooking lesson

Pledge $500 or more

Catered lunch for 12 people
Free item per day for 6 months
Backer names a menu item
2 hour cooking lesson for 3 people

Pledge $1000 or more

Catered lunch for 25 people
Personal chef service for a weekend

In the food truck business, you may or may not have any physical merchandise to sell. That's ok! Hats and T-shirts are common merchandise items as well as condiments and sauces. But when you don't have merchandise to give away, you'll have to reward backers with food and experiences… unless those merchandise items will be created after you launch your food truck. Many offer free meals in varying quantities as well as larger rewards like private catering for top contributing backers. The important thing to remember is to keep the reward close to its actual value… and only offer rewards you are comfortable giving away.

Rewarding Out of Town Backers

A lot of the rewards listed above are great for local backers especially when there are free entrees or catering offered. But keep in mind that you will have out of town backers that do not live near you. They still need to be rewarded also. In those cases, you might have increase the number of T-shirts, stickers or other merchandise you'll be sending out. Be sure to indicate how and what out of town backers will receive when they support your project.

Take a look at how Lexie's Frozen Custard Truck addressed backers that did not live near her location:

Pledge $10 or more

A card good for 3 scoops of our seasonal flavors. For out of state donations, we'll send you a set of handmade penguin note cards featuring a collage with the Lexie's penguin from our logo. Estimated delivery: Oct 2012.

Pledge $20 or more

A card good for 6 scoops of our seasonal flavors. For out of state donations, we'll send you a gift basket with penguin note cards and handmade sundae toppings. Estimated delivery: Oct 2012.

Pledge $50 or more

10-scoop card plus 2 pints of frozen custard. For out of state donations, we'll send you a gift basket with penguin note cards, handmade sundae toppings and baked treats. Estimated delivery: Aug 2012.

Pledge $100 or more

20-scoop card, 2 pints of frozen custard and a Lexie's Frozen Custard penguin T-shirt. For out of state donations, you'll get a custom made gift basket that will include notecards, handmade sundae toppings, baked treats, and 2 pints of frozen custard mailed to you! Estimated delivery: Oct 2012.

Pledge $500 or more

50-scoop card, T-shirt, 5 pints of frozen custard and personalized frozen party cake for up to 50 people. Out-of-state backers will receive 2 personalized frozen party cakes for up to 50 people each mailed to them at a date of their choice, plus a custom gift basket that will include notecards, handmade sundae toppings, baked treats, and 2 pints of frozen custard. Estimated delivery: Oct 2012.

Pledge $1000 or more

50-scoop card, T-shirt, 10 pints of frozen custard, personalized party cake and the truck for 3 hours at your special event with sundaes for up to 50 people. Out-of-state backers will receive 4 personalized frozen party cakes for up to 50 people mailed to them at a date of their choice, plus a custom gift basket that will include notecards, handmade sundae toppings, baked treats, and 2 pints of frozen custard. Estimated delivery: Oct 2012.

Notice how every single one of their rewards had a contingency for out of town or out of state backers. Not everyone does that! However, this probably helped their Kickstarter project succeed by appealing to backers from afar.

Lexie's Frozen Custard Truck ran their Kickstarter campaign for 2 weeks and generated $6280 from 75 backers. That comes out to 104% over their $6000 goal. The inclusion of out of town backers means you'll have a larger "crowd" of people to enlist support from than just the people in your vicinity!

Additional Reward Statistics

According to Kickstarter, the most popular contribution amount is $25. That's because it doesn't sound like too much or too little. However, the average contribution amount is about $70. So you should put more focus on the smaller reward levels. Think about your rewards as if you were a backer. What would make you want to back your project?

Here are some more amazing statistics about rewards that can help you create a better Kickstarter project:

Projects <u>without</u> a reward less than $20
Succeed 28% of the time

Projects <u>with</u> a reward of $20 or less
Succeed 45% of the time

Those are pretty compelling numbers to get project owners focusing more on the lower value rewards as they help to boost chances of getting fully funded! There's no real science to this but hopefully these statistics help guide you in setting up your rewards!

Reward Delivery Date

The last item to determine with your reward is the delivery date. This is simply when a backer can expect to receive their reward. This isn't an exact date. You'll have to figure out when you think you can realistically start distributing rewards. Again, this is an estimate and is displayed as "Estimated Delivery Date" after each reward.

Chapter 7 – Producing Your Video

Your video will probably be the first thing people click on when they visit your project page. This means you need to have a great looking video as part of your campaign. Your video is going to be the most effective way to communicate your true emotions when it comes to your business. It can explain the details of your business in a way that your written description can't!

A video is much more dynamic than just written words and still images. Personalities can come out in video that show off the dedication and emotion of the owners. The natural sounds and music and help further sell your idea to backers.

And even if you spent a lot of time writing out a detailed description of your project, there are going to be people who will never read it because they're lazy. A video is going to appeal to more people than just written words... especially online!

Why Video Should Be Mandatory

Posting a video in your Kickstarter project should not be an option! It SHOULD BE a requirement! When you look at project success rates, you'll see why a video is not something you should leave out!

Projects <u>with</u> videos
50% success rate

Projects <u>without</u> videos
30% success rate

Your video can be simple or elaborate. You can do it yourself or have someone produce it for you. Just make it creative and real! It doesn't have to be perfect but it should tell a good story about you and what you want to accomplish.

What to Include in Your Video

No matter the style of video you create for your project, there are some key elements that need to be included to make it a persuasive and effective video. One of the first things that should be included in the video is YOU! If the thought of being in front of the camera is intimidating, you're not alone! But this is one time where you do not want to shy away from putting yourself in front of the camera. This is your project. Your dream! And backers want to see the real person behind it! You should be the one delivering the message.

Look at it as having a conversation with a friend. Shoot it interview style where someone off camera asks you questions. And don't worry about messing up. You'll have plenty of chances to reshoot. Spend some time practicing being in front of the camera before the real shoot. These are the basic talking points you need to include in your video:

Tell the audience who you are
Explain your mission/dream
Where did your idea come from?
How will the money help you?
Where will the money be spent?
Current status of your business
Call to action for backer's support
Describe your rewards
Describe your menu
What if you fail to reach your funding goal?
Express your gratitude

Those are just the talking points. And in addition to having you on camera, you'll want plenty of B-roll shots. These are shots of other imagery related to your talking points. If you're talking about needing funds to repair an old food truck you just purchased, then shoot video of that truck. If you mention certain menu items, then shoot video of you preparing and serving those items. And if it's any help to calm your on-camera performance fears, listen to this. By having a lot of B-roll shots, your face will not be on-camera the whole time in the video!

Don't think that this video thing has to be a huge production. It doesn't. Some videos are as simple as turning on the camera and just telling your story to the lens. The whole thing could be shot on a single day! However, it's not difficult to get professional looking video with today's technology.

Finding an Inexpensive Videographer

If you're going to be a food truck owner, chances are, you are also a do-it-yourself type of person. When producing your video, you could have a friend or significant other help you shoot it. But there are other options if you want a more professional look and feel. You might think finding a specialist will cost a fortune but it doesn't have to!

Today's camera technology is affordable for a lot of people which means you have more choices to pick from when looking for a good videographer. Here are some ideas where you can find an inexpensive videographer:

Friends
Students
Art Schools
Craigslist
Co-workers
Churches

The truth is that you can realistically find students in high school that can produce professional looking videos that rival those that have years of experience. A lot of times, students will take on video projects for free or very little money just for the experience. But just like offering rewards to your backers, you should compensate your videographer somehow even if they don't charge you.

Type of Camera to Use

These days, you can get great looking HD video from your mobile phone or compact digital camera. A lot of times this is great if you're doing it yourself. But, if you hire a student or a part-time videographer, chances are that they will be using a DSLR camera to shoot your video. Shooting video with DSLRs has become extremely popular and common. The reason is that a variety of lenses can be used to get cinema-style looks to the video. This adds to the professional look of the entire video.

With a DSLR, a shallow depth-of-field can be achieved. This means that if the camera is focused on you in the shot, the background will be blurred.

All current DSLR cameras shoot up to 1080p HD video and would be perfect for producing a Kickstarter video. An example of a popular DSLR used for video is the Canon EOS 7D. But as mentioned before, a DSLR is not necessary. But if you do end up hiring someone to shoot and edit your video, it's well worth finding someone who knows how to shoot video with a DSLR camera.

Music and Video Formats

Adding a music track to your Kickstarter video can really enhance the message and give it feeling. Music isn't necessary but it definitely helps. Most of the time, a videographer will have his or her own collection of production music or can get access to some. But be careful with the music you choose! Don't use copyrighted music in your video without permission.

You could get sued and fined. If you need help on where to find music, here's a list:

MusicBakery.com
PremiumBeat.com
Vimeo.com/musicstore
cc.Mixter.org
FreeMusicArchive.org

Some of those sites offer free tracks while others sell premium tracks. But even with the free tracks, you need to read the license agreement and terms of use for each track. Some are not allowed for commercial use.

Kickstarter allows you to upload you video in a variety of formats. These are the most common formats used in the video production industry. Most editing programs can output some if not all the following file types:

MOV
AVI
MPEG
MP4
WMV
FLV
3GP

In addition to those format requirements, your video needs to be 1000mb or less before uploading. There's really no set length for your video but you should aim for about the 3 to 7 minute range so viewers don't get bored.

An excellent example of a professional looking Kickstarter video is the one from Renny's Oki Doki Okinawan Food Truck.

http://www.kickstarter.com/projects/1604060644/rennys-oki-doki-okinawan-food-truck-launch?ref=live

The Oki Doki video pretty much embraces everything that should be included in an effective Kickstarter video. It's not necessarily perfect but it looks good and tells a very compelling story. They incorporated a lot of B-roll and photos. The music definitely helps and they filmed the owner in 2 different settings (both with the truck).

Use the Oki Doki video as a guide but be sure to put in your own personal touches and personality to really make it special!

Why Post Your Video Elsewhere?

In addition to having your video appear on your project page, you should upload your video to other online video hosting services. This will give your video more exposure. Here's a list of free online video hosting services:

YouTube
Vimeo
Google Videos
Dailymotion
MetaCafe
Yahoo Videos

There are so many free video sites you could use but the ones listed above are some of the most well-known and popular. Be sure to include a description of your project when you upload to those services and also include a link to your Kickstarter project page when writing your video description. In addition, you should add the words "Kickstarter video" somewhere in your video title when uploading to a video site. This will get picked up in the search engines and your video may show up in various searches for Kickstarter related content.

Chapter 8 – Launching and Promoting Your Project

Once you have your account set up, your description written, a funding goal set, rewards identified and a compelling video produced, you're ready to launch your project! However, it doesn't end there! Once your project is launched, how are you going to get backers to support you? This is where you're going to need to do some promotion. Support can come from anywhere but the majority of it will most likely come from your own network of contacts and the friends of those contacts.

You need to reach out and tell everyone about your Kickstarter campaign! Some of this should be done in the days before your actual launch. Starting out with a simple, personal message to friends and family should be your first step. These individuals will usually be the first backers of your project. This initial push will let potential backers know that others have already backed your project. Once people see that a project is starting to gain momentum, they're more likely to join in.

How to Get Initial Backers

Once you've contacted your immediate network of friends and family, you'll need to really scale up your promotion efforts to people you don't know. This is where you need to start using social media and the internet. Facebook and Twitter are the natural choice for this. You need to send out reminders on a regular basis to keep your project fresh on the minds of potential backers. You'll have to create a balance of not sending too many messages but you also don't want to send too few. Remember your project is going to run for about 30 days so you have plenty of time to get the word out!

If you have a blog, you should also start writing blog posts about your Kickstarter campaign. You never know when an existing or random reader will take interest in your project. A lot of times, Kickstarter pages get indexed in Google and other search engines where you may end up picking up a few more backers.

Automating Your Promotional Updates

Promoting your project requires constant maintenance. However, when it comes to your reminder messages through social media, there are ways to make it easier by automating. Wouldn't it be nice to have some of those messages sent out for you while you're doing other things? It's not recommended to automate all of your social media efforts. But if you happen to be working a full-time job or have a busy schedule, automating can help you keep the news of your project fresh with your followers.

One of the best tools for social media automation is Hootsuite. It's a free online platform that allows you to link and manage all your social media accounts in one location. It allows for immediate delivery of your messages but the Twitter automation is ultimately what you will want to use it for.

This can be a huge timesaver! You could essentially look at a calendar and pre-compose messages that correspond to each day of your campaign. For example, if it's the 10th day of your campaign, you could schedule a message written like this:

> "We're 10 days into our campaign but we still need your support to help us reach our funding goal! Help us make this happen!"

At the end of each message, you should provide a link to your Kickstarter page. Hootsuite can automatically shrink website links to allow you more room to type your message. Their shortened links are automatically tracked so you can see if people are clicking on those links to view your Kickstarter page.

Promoting Your Project Locally

Getting the word out online is relatively simple and easy. However, don't forget to do some legwork and promote locally and in-person. Try to get into meet-ups and organizations where you can explain your goal in person. Go to local farmers markets or events that are related to your theme. Attend food truck events and talk to customers. You can print up flyers and hand them out. Explain why your community needs your truck.

You can even host pledge parties to get local backers. Let them sample some of your food to further entice their interest. Don't be afraid to contact local media and tell them about your story. Writing a press release and sending it out to local media outlets can't hurt either. The free coverage you get from local radio and TV stations could greatly help you reach your funding goal.

How to Get Into Local Media

Here's a word of advice for soliciting to local media. Make sure you present a story idea that has a local hook to it. That's what the local media outlets are looking for. For example, if you know you are the first and only paleo based food truck in your city, make sure you include that in your press release. Or maybe tie in your promotion efforts with a local event that you know will get press coverage.

You should also target writers that cover local food and lifestyle stories. You are much more likely to appeal to them than someone who covers politics or crime. Also, reach out to local food and event bloggers. They have their own audience of followers where you can pick up a few more backers. Just try not to be an annoyance to them!

The same rules apply when you're contacting local media. Don't hound them too much! If you're seen as annoying, you're guaranteed to be rejected. Speaking of rejection, don't get upset if you don't hear back from the media. You have to understand that they are constantly being bombarded by people like you who are looking for some coverage. They are limited with time and space when it comes to the stories they will cover.

Because most people can't resist free food, one strategy would be to invite the media to a tasting event. If you get even one reporter to show up, you will most likely be able to have a decent conversation with them to see if they're interested in your story.

When you're in the promotion stage of your project, just have fun with it! This is where you get to connect with people and show your passion for what you're doing! This is where you get to express the real you to real people.

Providing Project Updates

After your project is live, another task you need to stay on top of is your project updates. This is not only a part of your Kickstarter project page but also part of your promotion strategy as well. Kickstarter gives you the ability to post updates on your status via the Updates tab on your Kickstarter page. This is where you will be posting news, milestones, gratitude and anything else you want to say to your backers.

The Updates area functions just like a blog. You can post your article there, insert pictures, links and embed video clips. Readers can also make comments that you can respond to. Your updates can help create momentum and excitement during your campaign.

Provide status updates on funding. Here, you can announce daily or weekly goals you want to reach with your funding. Use techniques employed by telethons by saying something like:

"We only need $250 more to reach today's goal of $2000! Let's make it happen!"

This is also an area where you can share your thoughts and thank people who have already contributed. Posting update videos with a personal message can also help people relate to your excitement about your project. These don't have to be long videos. Just turn on the camera and talk for 30 seconds!

How to Get More Than 100% Funding

Every project is going to be different. Some will get full funding early while others will get fully funded at the very last minute. However, if you find you have reached your funding goal early, don't stop there! Those extra days in your campaign can be used to capture funds over and above your original funding goal!

How do you do this? Instead of just saying thank you and leaving the project alone, this is where you should announce a second funding goal. Now this goal is not part of your original Kickstarter campaign but rather an impromptu attempt to utilize the remaining days you have available before your project closes.

Of course, when you do reach your original funding goal, you should absolutely pour your heart out and thank everyone who supported you! Next, you will announce that because there's time left, you are going to try to achieve a second funding goal. Don't make this goal too high but any extra funds could come in handy to help pay off your startup expenses. You should also explain what the extra funds will be used for if you are successful at reaching this second goal.

After you've set this second goal, go back through the initial steps of promotion and tell everyone about it! However, this time, you can leave out the part about contacting the local media. Again, have fun with this second phase of your promotion and enjoy what extra funding you can get!

Chapter 9 – Successful Funding! What Next?

Once your project is complete and you are successful, you need to start sending out thank you messages to your backers. Let them know how much you appreciate them for helping you achieve your goal! These final updates should be sent through all your online accounts like Twitter and Facebook. But be sure to create final updates on your Kickstarter page as well.

It doesn't hurt to shoot a short video with a personal message expressing your appreciation directly addressing your backers. Your emotions and joy should show through here! Post this on all your social media accounts as well. Once you've thanked all your backers, your job is not over yet!

Now you need to take the funds you worked so hard to raise and put it to use and launch your food truck business! That is going to be quite a task and hopefully you can stop worrying about the financial aspect for a while. But even when your food truck is ready, there's still the task of distributing rewards to your backers!

Reward Fulfillment

Reward fulfillment is the part where you deliver your promised rewards to your backers. Hopefully you can start distributing near the date of your Estimated Delivery Date. If you think there is going to be a delay on the delivery date, then you should send out another update announcing a new estimated time. This portion of your Kickstarter project can easily be an overwhelming task. This is where being organized can really help. To prepare to deliver your rewards, you may need to start stocking up on some of these items:

Boxes
Envelopes
Bubble wrap
Stamps
Business cards
Packing tape
Custom printed items
Labels
More!

Obviously the supplies you need will depend on what you are delivering. For food truck businesses, most rewards are meal related so you may have to print up certificates that your backers can use when they claim their rewards.

Take into account shipping costs as well as the cost of purchasing the mailing supplies. When it's all said and done, it could take a couple of weeks to ship out all your rewards! Depending on the number of backers you have, it could take you more or less time to fulfill. For Kickstarter food truck projects, the average number of backers is 137 when last checked.

How to Collect Contact Info from Backers

During the course of your project, you will not have much, if any information about your backers. There is absolutely no need to worry about this information before your project ends. But if your project is successfully funded, you will need to use the Kickstarter Survey Tool to gather this data. This tool will help you create surveys which are designed to gather any information you need to deliver your rewards. You can request information such as:

Addresses
Quantity
Color desired
Sizes
Alternate rewards
Phone numbers
More!

The Kickstarter Survey Tool is found in your Backer Report. When you send out the survey, backers will receive an email with instructions on how to get their information to you. Once a backer has entered the necessary data, this information will be automatically saved in the Backer Report. Once you've gathered enough responses to start processing the rewards, you can export the data to an Excel spreadsheet and print out the results. Now you have a checklist you can easily work from.

Post Final Updates When Distributing Rewards

Again, this is another opportunity to reassure your backers that they will be receiving their reward soon. Explain your experience whether good or bad while putting together reward packages. Take lots of photos and maybe even shoot some videos of the whole process. This way, backers can see your project all the way to the end. This is also a good way for you to keep a record of your project from start to finish. Completed Kickstarter projects remain on their website so you can always go back and reminisce about your experience!

This really is the final stage of your Kickstarter project and you should be proud of what you've accomplished! Starting a crowdfunding project on Kickstarter can be an up and down roller coaster ride which can cause a lot of joy and frustration. But it is well worth it if you need financial help launching a mobile food business!

What If a Project is Unsuccessful?

It's a fact that more than 50% of funding projects are unsuccessful. But using the techniques in this book can give you an advantage. But what do you do if your project is unsuccessful? This can certainly be a set-back. However, Kickstarter allows you to post your project again in another attempt to raise the money you need. However, you probably don't want to run your projects back to back. If you run your project again too soon, you may end up with fewer backers than before! It's best to let some time pass before starting up again. Of course that's going to completely delay your food truck launch deadline (if you have one). But reposting a project does work!

Lexie's Frozen Custard in San Francisco ran 2 Kickstarter projects in an attempt to get their truck on the road. They were unsuccessful on their first attempt. Here's some information from their first Kickstarter project:

Project #1
Launched: February 15, 2012
Ended: April 15, 2012
Funding Goal: $20,000
Backers: 59
Amount Pledged: $8921

Let's analyze their project so we can see what could be improved. They did have a video with a personal message in it from the owner, Alexis LeCount. She also had a good selection of rewards for backers but a very short written description of their project. Most of it looks ok but the most probable cause of their failure was that their funding goal was too high and she ran her project for the full 60 days. Now let's take a look at Alexis' second Kickstarter project and compare the differences.

Project #2
Launched: June 9, 2012
Ended: June 24, 2012
Funding Goal: $6,000
Backers: 75
Amount Pledged: $6280

In her second project, she used the same video and continued with another short project description. However, she only ran the project for 14 days and set a funding goal of about 1/3 of what she asked for in the first campaign. It's amazing that she was able to reach this second goal in such a short period of time! She waited 2 months in between projects before posting the project again. However, in that 2 month period, she was able to secure some funds from another source which allowed her to set a smaller Kickstarter funding goal the second time around.

Conclusion

Now it's time for you to start putting together your own Kickstarter project! Remember to start planning long before you intend to launch. And don't forget to start practicing on-camera for your video. Patience and personality can go a long way in this business. And if you don't succeed, there are second chances! But overall, just have fun with the whole process and you may end up with an experience that <u>can</u> change your life!

Bonus: Food Truck Successes on Kickstarter

Two Blokes and a Bus
Funding Goal: $15,000
Amount Pledged: $17,886
Percent Funded: 119%
Project Duration: 30 days
Number of Backers: 138

Benaddiction
Funding Goal: $20,000
Amount Pledged: $20,330
Percent Funded: 101%
Project Duration: 30 days
Number of Backers: 145

The Pastrami Project
Funding Goal: $10,000
Amount Pledged: $10,136
Percent Funded: 101%
Project Duration: 30 days
Number of Backers: 59

The Grilled Cheese Bus
Funding Goal: $8,000

Amount Pledged: $8,788
Percent Funded: 109%
Project Duration: 30 days
Number of Backers: 183

The Reuben Truck
Funding Goal: $15,000
Amount Pledged: $15,432
Percent Funded: 102%
Project Duration: 30 days
Number of Backers: 160

Lexie's Frozen Custard
Funding Goal: $6,000
Amount Pledged: $6,280
Percent Funded: 104%
Project Duration: 14 days
Number of Backers: 75

Friar Tuck's Truck
Funding Goal: $3,000
Amount Pledged: $3,701
Percent Funded: 105%
Project Duration: 30 days
Number of Backers: 31

The DipStik Bus
Funding Goal: $13,000
Amount Pledged: $13,727
Percent Funded: 105%
Project Duration: 30 days
Number of Backers: 44

Grind
Funding Goal: $5,000
Amount Pledged: $5,961
Percent Funded: 108%
Project Duration: 45 days
Number of Backers: 105

La Empanada
Funding Goal: $7,500
Amount Pledged: $7,699
Percent Funded: 102%
Project Duration: 30 days
Number of Backers: 116

Big Wheel
Funding Goal: $6,000
Amount Pledged: $6,837
Percent Funded: 124%
Project Duration: 30 days
Number of Backers: 98

Mother Juice
Funding Goal: $14,000
Amount Pledged: $14,443
Percent Funded: 111%
Project Duration: 30 days
Number of Backers: 234

Outside the Box
Funding Goal: $20,000

Amount Pledged: $22,196
Percent Funded: 110%
Project Duration: 45 days
Number of Backers: 232

Tailgate
Funding Goal: $13,000
Amount Pledged: $13,025
Percent Funded: 100%
Project Duration: 37 days
Number of Backers: 46

The Fisherman's Dog
Funding Goal: $7,000
Amount Pledged: $7,300
Percent Funded: 104%
Project Duration: 30 days
Number of Backers: 128

Not So Fast!
Funding Goal: $7,000
Amount Pledged: $7,405
Percent Funded: 114%
Project Duration: 30 days
Number of Backers: 219

Renny's Oki Doki
Funding Goal: $4,500
Amount Pledged: $10,232
Percent Funded: 227%
Project Duration: 14 days
Number of Backers: 110

314 PIE

Funding Goal: $10,000
Amount Pledged: $12,346
Percent Funded: 123%
Project Duration: 30 days
Number of Backers: 300

French Indo

Funding Goal: $3,700
Amount Pledged: $3,950
Percent Funded: 106%
Project Duration: 30 days
Number of Backers: 64

Lloyd Taco Truck

Funding Goal: $12,500
Amount Pledged: $13,741
Percent Funded: 109%
Project Duration: 30 days
Number of Backers: 299

Radish

Funding Goal: $5,250
Amount Pledged: $5,860
Percent Funded: 111%
Project Duration: 30 days
Number of Backers: 95

Fueled by Fries

Funding Goal: $10,000

Amount Pledged: $10,116
Percent Funded: 101%
Project Duration: 30 days
Number of Backers: 180

The Wagyu Wagon
Funding Goal: $10,000
Amount Pledged: $10,100
Percent Funded: 101%
Project Duration: 40 days
Number of Backers: 51

CCB Food Truck
Funding Goal: $12,000
Amount Pledged: $12,230
Percent Funded: 101%
Project Duration: 90 days
Number of Backers: 159

Morel's Vegan Food Truck
Funding Goal: $12,000
Amount Pledged: $13,002
Percent Funded: 108%
Project Duration: 60 days
Number of Backers: 220

Lebanese Street Food
Funding Goal: $8,000
Amount Pledged: $8,851
Percent Funded: 110%
Project Duration: 45 days
Number of Backers: 154

Good Food Truck

Funding Goal: $4,200

Amount Pledged: $4,410

Percent Funded: 105%

Project Duration: 45 days

Number of Backers: 76

For more information about starting your own food truck, please visit:

FoodTruckBusinessPlan.com

Would You Like to Know More?

Learn more about the food truck industry and what it takes to start your own food truck business with the other titles in the Food Truck Startup series.

The best part is that I frequently run special promotions and discount my books (usually $0.99 USD). It's a great way to save and learn about this unique career path.

The best way to get notified of these deals is to subscribe to my Entrepreneur's Book Club. It's free to join and you'll also get a copy of **Food Truck Vehicles and Equipment**. This free guide will introduce you to some of the components and systems found on food trucks as well as details on the actual vehicles.

Please visit the following URL to get promotion updates and download the free book:

TheFoodTruckStartup.com/free

Did you like this book?

I'd like to say thank you for purchasing my book. My goal is to provide the most complete information about food trucks and the industry. I hope you enjoyed it!
As a favor, I would be grateful if you could take a minute and please leave me a review for this book at the website you purchased it from. Your feedback will help me to continue writing and updating the information about the food truck industry.

Thank you!
Andrew Moorehouse

Blog: FoodTruckBusinessPlan.com
Books: TheFoodTruckStartup.com

Made in the USA
San Bernardino, CA
16 December 2016